M000166115

PLAIDYPUS LOST

Janet
Stevens
and
Susan
Stevens
Crummel

For The Bridge Group,
my YaYas for the past 30 years—
Susan, Emily, Peggy, Nancy, Brenda,
Harriett, and Robin
S.S.C.

For my son Blake and
his often lost stuffed platypus
J.S.

Plaidypus Lost by Janet Stevens and Susan Stevens Crummel.
Text copyright © 2004 by Janet Stevens and Susan Stevens Crummel.
Illustrations copyright © 2004 by Janet Stevens.
All rights reserved. Reprinted by permission of Holiday House, Inc.

Little Book version of *Plaidypus Lost* published by Scott Foresman.

ISBN: 0-328-19158-2

3 4 5 6 7 8 9 10 V008 12 11 10

Plaidypus lost.
Plaidypus found.
This story goes around
and around.

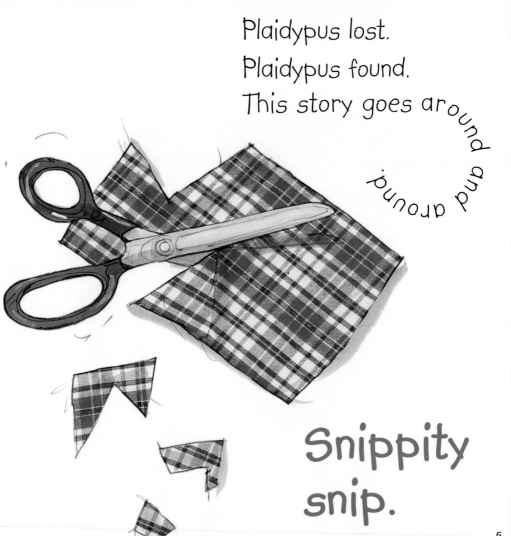

Snippity
snip.

Stitchity
stitch.

6

Buttons for eyes.

Surprise!

Grandpa's old plaid shirt
is now my new

PLAIDYPUS!

Thanks, Grandma.
I'll never lose him.

Off to the park.
Run to the slide.

11

Jump on the swing.

Back

and
forth.

In.　　Out.

OUCH!

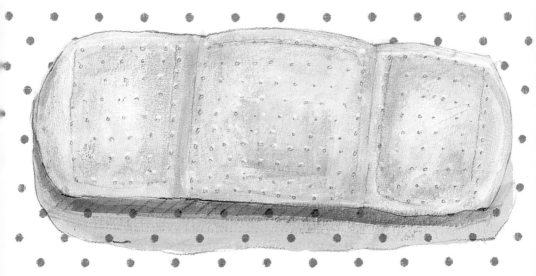

Fix my knee
at Grandma's house.

Uh-oh.

Where's Plaidypus?
Look left. Look right.
Nowhere in sight.
Back at the park.
Search high and low.
Over. Under.

Where did he go?

I think I *see* something
stuck in the sand.
A big plaid head
and a little webbed hand!

I'm sorry, Plaidypus.
I'll never, ever lose you again.

Plaidypus lost.
Plaidypus found.
This story goes

around
and around

Off to the market.
Push the big cart.
Fast and slow.
Stop. Go.

Candy in.

Candy out.

Pack up the groceries.
Load up the car.
Unload. Unpack.
Fold up the sacks.

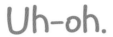

Uh-oh.
Where's Plaidypus?
Look left. Look right.
Nowhere in sight.

Back at the market.
Search high and low.
Over. Under.

Where did
he go?

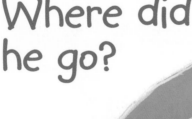

I think I see something up on a shelf.
How did he get there all by himself?

I'm sorry, Plaidypus.

I'll never, ever, ever lose you again.

Plaidypus lost.

Plaidypus found.

This story goes around and around

Off to the lake.
Go for a swim.

A snorkel for me.
A snorkel for him.

Into the water.
Out of the water.
Wet. Dry.
Sink. Float.

Hey!

There's my buddy
who lives down
the street.
Look at
these flippers.
Here on my feet!

Splashing attack!

Afternoon snack.

A cookie for you,
a cookie for me, a cookie for . . .

Uh-oh.

Where's Plaidypus?
Look left. Look right.
Nowhere in sight.
Back in the lake.
Search high and low.
Over. Under.

Where did he go?

Here comes
a fisherman.
EVERYONE,
LOOK!

I think I see
something
caught on
his hook.

I'm sorry, Plaidypus.

I'll never, ever,
ever, ever
lose you again.

Plaidypus lost.
Plaidypus found.
This story goes
around
and around

Off on a trip.
Ride in the car.
Window up. Window down.
In. Out. **Plaidypus flies!**

Car hits a bump.

THUMP!
Uh-oh.

Where's Plaidypus?
Look left. Look right.
Nowhere in sight.

Back down the road.
Search high and low.
Over. Under.

Where did he go?

Here in a bush?
There on a rock?
Up in a tree?
Where can he be?
It's getting dark.
We have to go.

I know!

I'll make a sign that people can see.

Someone will find him and bring him to me.

Missing
Plaidypus
Please return to
Grandma's house
112
Oak St.

One day. Two days.

Three days.

Four.

Finally, a knock at the door!
Look left. Look right.
No one in sight.
I think I *see* something
there in a sack.
What can it *be?*
My *best* friend is back!

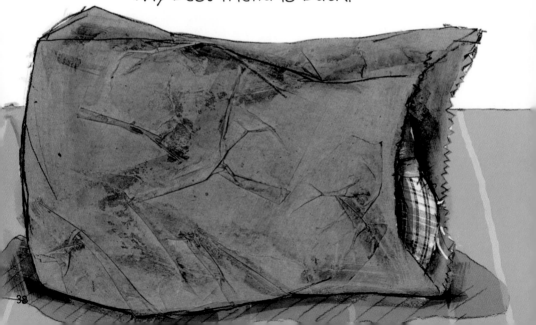

I'm sorry, Plaidypus.

I'll never, ever, ever, ever, ever
lose you again.

Plaidypus lost.
Plaidypus found.
This story goes
around
and around.

But Grandma, he's hurt.
Look at this tear.
One eye is missing.
An arm isn't there.
Can you fix him, please?

Snippity snip.
Stitchity stitch.
Striped patches.
Polka dots, too.
Surprise!

That old Plaidypus
is now my new one-eyed, one-armed

PLAIDA-
POLKA-
STRIPAPUS!

And I promise
I'll never, ever,

ever,

ever,

ever,

ever

lose you
again.

The
End

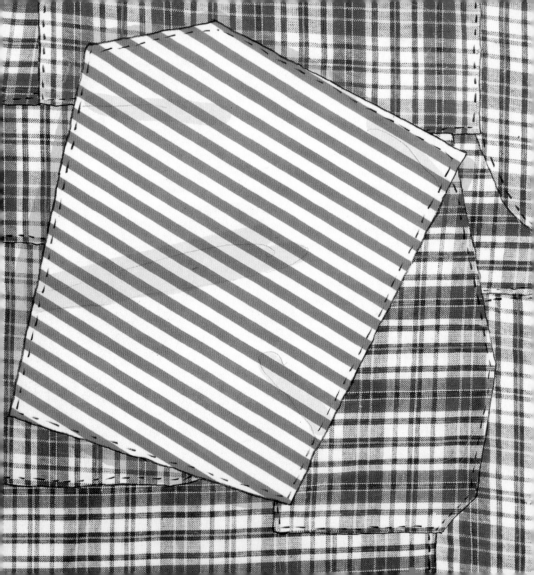